DIFFERENT DRUMMERS

How Teachers of Teachers
View Public Education

A Report from Public Agenda

By Steve Farkas and Jean Johnson
With Ann Duffett

Consulting Editor: Chris Perry

ABOUT PUBLIC AGENDA

Founded in 1975 by social scientist and author Daniel Yankelovich and former U.S. Secretary of State Cyrus Vance, Public Agenda works to help average citizens better understand critical policy issues and to help the nation's leaders better understand the public's point of view. Public Agenda's in-depth research on how average citizens think about policy forms the basis for extensive citizen education work. Its citizen education materials, used by the National Issues Forums and media outlets across the country, have won praise for their credibility and fairness from elected officials from both political parties and from experts and decision-makers across the political spectrum.

ACKNOWLEDGMENTS

The authors of *Different Drummers* would like to thank these individuals for their support and assistance during the preparation of this report:

Public Agenda's Communications Director, Margaret Suzor Dunning, and her associates Vincent Calabrese and Sara Clough, who skillfully bring our work to the attention of a broad audience.

Our Public Agenda colleagues Michael Buryk, Joanna Cohen, Caroline Corbin, Will Friedman, Michael deCourcy Hinds, Steve Immerwahr, Kathie Johnson, Zarela Maldonado, Joanna McHugh, Keith Melville, Janet Polokoff, Alex Trilling, and David White, who are always willing to lend their good humor, support, knowledge, and creativity.

David G. Imig, Chief Executive Officer of the American Association of Colleges for Teacher Education, who provided thoughtful counsel and gracious assistance throughout the research process.

Daniel Yankelovich, who joined with Cyrus Vance more than two decades ago to found Public Agenda. Dan's insights and his wisdom provide the intellectual backbone of our work.

Deborah Wadsworth, Public Agenda's Executive Director, whose energy and intelligence, deep belief in education, and ongoing support made this project possible.

DIFFERENT DRUMMERS

How Teachers of Teachers
View Public Education

A REPORT FROM PUBLIC AGENDA

**Funding for this project was provided by the
Thomas B. Fordham Foundation.**

ISBN: 1-889483-47-8

TABLE OF CONTENTS

In the summer of 1997, many Americans sat before their TV sets mesmerized by live pictures of the planet Mars served up by NASA's Mars Pathfinder mission. Those concerned about the state of American education may also have been captivated by another aspect of the broadcasts: a parade of capable and articulate scientists and engineers who personified the traits that most of us – whatever our specific views on education – expect our schools to produce.

These scientists and engineers clearly knew "their stuff." They commanded an impressive store of detailed, factual knowledge and put it to use with an accuracy and precision well beyond that expected in many professions. They displayed the values that many of us want our educators to emphasize – they were persistent and hardworking, able to face setbacks without giving up. At the same time, they had the creativity and resourcefulness to solve devilishly complex problems, and they were obviously thrilled by their chance to explore the unknown. Here, on display for all to see, were men and women who possessed knowledge, discipline, and an unmistakable, almost contagious, love of learning.

THE FRUITS OF EDUCATION

Few would disagree that these traits are the hoped-for fruits of education, whether the field is science, business, government, or the arts. But there is significant disagreement on how schools and teachers should achieve these results. The public, alarmed by what it sees as a widespread lack of skills and motivation in today's students, advocates a time-honored approach: Teach children how to read and write; help them master grammar and spelling; teach them to calculate; give them the story of their country's history; and help them develop diligence and self-discipline. And while they're at it, passing on a few manners wouldn't hurt either.

To the public, teaching children to master these "basics" is putting first things first. Students will then be free to achieve and explore – to make whatever they can of themselves.

But others question the public's approach, fearing that its emphasis on basics, discipline, and traditional teaching methods will not produce the inventive, flexible thinking that modern times demand. For this group, educators must use new strategies and teaching techniques better suited to a rapidly changing world. These strategies and techniques include: emphasizing problem-solving exercises; critical thinking skills; use of the Internet and other tools to find and process information; teaching students to work in groups; and, perhaps most important, teaching children to "learn how to learn."

WHAT WORKS

These general philosophies about what works have real consequences. Inevitably, they lead to differences in what teachers and students do on a daily basis – what students are exposed to, how they are motivated, how teachers plan and conduct lessons, how they judge a student's progress, how schools are organized, and how we as a society measure success. Deciding what creates an educated person is at the core of many, if not most, debates about the public schools.

TEACHERS OF TEACHERS

Over the past several years, Public Agenda has explored the perspectives of parents, teachers, students, leaders, and the general public on many aspects of this very question. Now we turn our attention – and our research – to a group that, perhaps more than any other, is in the business of defining what education is and should be: professors of education from America's colleges and universities – the teachers of our teachers.

Their convictions and beliefs, it seems, should have particular significance since they are the source of a chain reaction. Assuming that they are at least reasonably effective, what education professors teach about learning and schools shapes the goals, expectations, and priorities of the nation's teacher corps. At the same time, what they don't teach either doesn't get learned or must be learned on the job.

> **What education professors teach about learning and schools shapes the goals, expectations, and priorities of the nation's teacher corps.**

THE RESEARCH

To find out what the teachers of teachers think about education and the public schools, Public Agenda surveyed by telephone 900 professors of education during the summer of 1997. Before designing the survey, Public Agenda interviewed a number of education experts and opinion leaders to obtain their suggestions for interesting lines of inquiry, and conducted focus groups with education professors in four cities – New York, Chicago, Boston, and Los Angeles.

> **Some readers will undoubtedly be infuriated by the professors' views, while others will be heartened by them.**

Public Agenda would particularly like to thank the Thomas B. Fordham Foundation, which provided underwriting for the study. As with all such projects, Public Agenda is solely responsible for determining the lines of inquiry, designing the questionnaire, and interpreting and reporting research results.

Public Agenda's 1997 study of high school students (*Getting By: What American Teenagers Really Think About Their Schools*) found teens unequivocal in saying that classroom teachers have the most significant impact on their desire and ability to learn. But high school students are not alone in making the judgment that teachers are the center-piece of improved student learning. Virtually everyone agrees that good teachers are the most essential ingredient of good schools.

VOICES IN THE WILDERNESS?

As revealed in the following pages, professors of education have a distinctive, perhaps even singular, prescription for what good teachers should do – one that differs markedly from that of most parents and taxpayers. To a surprising extent, the professors' views also differ from those of most classroom teachers. Some readers will undoubtedly be infuriated by the professors' views, while others will be heartened by them. But what the professors say about education and teaching, and about children and learning, is important – arguably even obligatory – reading for anyone aiming to improve America's schools.

Teachers of teachers envision classrooms as places where teachers and students are active, life-long learners; education is a collaborative enterprise; and the process of struggling with questions is far more important than knowing the right answers.

THE SOUL OF A TEACHER

Education professors speak with passionate idealism about their own sometimes lofty vision of education and the mission of teacher education programs. That passion translates into ambitious and highly evolved expectations for future teachers, expectations that often differ dramatically from those of parents and teachers now in the classroom.

"The soul of a teacher is what should be passed on from teacher to teacher," a Boston professor said with some intensity. "You can be a life-long learner and learn the things you don't know in terms of the content, but you have to have that soul to be a good teacher." A Chicago professor outlined his vision in this way: "I expect [graduates of my program] to be able to think critically and process information, to be effective communicators, effective collaborators and cooperators. And finally, I expect them to have effective habits of mind – that they think for themselves and have some sense of identity."

DEFENDERS OF THE FAITH

Indeed, when asked how "absolutely essential" it is to impart a series of traits to prospective teachers, 84% of the education professors point to teachers "who are themselves life-long learners." Another 82% point to teachers "committed to teaching kids to be active learners" as a key trait to transmit to prospective teachers. These overwhelming majorities stand in sharp contrast to the 41% who believe it is absolutely essential to produce teachers "trained in pragmatic issues of running a classroom such as managing time and preparing lesson plans." Other qualities – such as expecting students to be neat, on time, and polite; or emphasizing correct spelling, grammar, and punctuation – draw even less support.

As will be detailed later in this report, the public's chief concerns lie precisely in these other areas. Prior Public Agenda studies have identified gaps in thinking between ordinary Americans and leaders or experts about a host of issues, but it is unusual to find disparities of this magnitude about such fundamental goals, and involving an issue – public education – that is so close to the public's heart.

Nor are these disparities confined to disagreement over broad education goals; they also appear when education professors describe where they invest their teaching energies when working with prospective teachers. For example, only 3 in 10 education professors (30%) say their teacher education programs emphasize teaching prospective teachers how to manage a rowdy classroom – a predicament many public school teachers, both new and veteran, say they face. Similarly, 3 in 4 members of the public (74%), and more than 8 in 10 teachers (82%), consider it absolutely essential to teach values such as honesty. Meanwhile, 68% of high school students say cheating on tests and assignments is a serious problem in their school.[1] But only 8% of education professors say their programs put a lot of emphasis on training teachers-to-be on how to handle such situations.

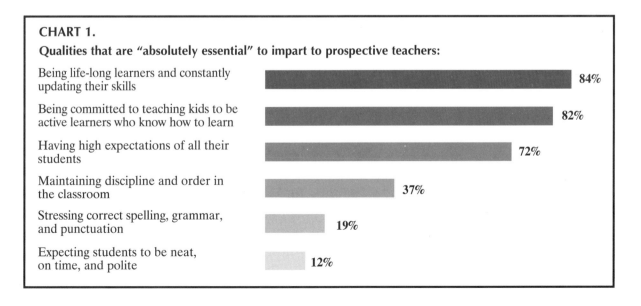

CHART 1.

Qualities that are "absolutely essential" to impart to prospective teachers:

Quality	Percent
Being life-long learners and constantly updating their skills	84%
Being committed to teaching kids to be active learners who know how to learn	82%
Having high expectations of all their students	72%
Maintaining discipline and order in the classroom	37%
Stressing correct spelling, grammar, and punctuation	19%
Expecting students to be neat, on time, and polite	12%

THE PROFESSOR'S PRESCRIPTION – ACTIVE LEARNING

Education professors have a clear response for how to deal with disorder and lack of discipline, which head the list of teacher and parent concerns. It is often when teachers fail to encourage active learning, the professors say, that they face order and discipline problems in their classrooms.

About 6 in 10 education professors (61%) believe that when a public school teacher faces a disruptive class, he or she has probably failed to make lessons engaging enough to capture the students' attention. "Effective motivation that turns kids on to learning is a positive way of dealing with discipline," said a Los Angeles professor, "and I think you need to do that instead of just controlling them." A Chicago professor said much the same thing: "We teach students how to become active learners, and I think that relates to the discipline problem...When you have students engaged and not vessels to receive information, you tend to have fewer discipline problems."

Underlying these attitudes seems to be a sense that children have an innate love of learning that can be used to harness any wayward or mischievous impulses. The belief that tapping into this innate love of learning will capture the devoted attention of students is powerful among education professors, so much so that many seem to question the need for academic sanctions. In fact, most professors of education (59%) believe that academic sanctions such as the threat of failing a course or being held back a grade are not an important part of motivating kids to learn. The age-old incentive kids have always had for studying and working hard in school – the fear of getting a bad grade – is unnecessary and inappropriate, the professors say.

PROCESS OVER CONTENT

The intellectual process of searching and struggling to learn is far more important to education professors than whether or not students ultimately master a particular set of facts. The primacy that process holds over outcomes is indicated by this finding: 86% of education professors say when K-12 teachers assign students math or history questions, it is more important for the kids to struggle with the process of seeking the right answers; only 12% consider it more important for kids to end up knowing the right answers.

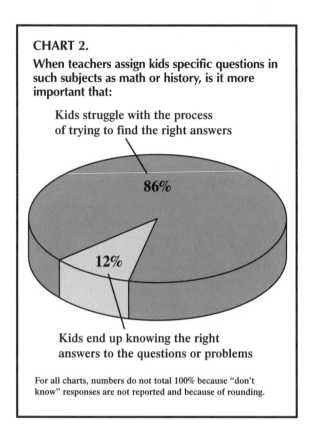

CHART 2.

When teachers assign kids specific questions in such subjects as math or history, is it more important that:

Kids struggle with the process of trying to find the right answers

86%

12%

Kids end up knowing the right answers to the questions or problems

For all charts, numbers do not total 100% because "don't know" responses are not reported and because of rounding.

As long as students know where to find the information they need and how to access it, many education professors reason, why force them to demonstrate knowledge of specific facts? In the focus groups, education professors often cited the availability of computers or calculators to illustrate their point that information is now available at people's fingertips – and no longer needs to be on the tip of their tongues.

"Giving people tools is probably more important than all of that information – which they can now get on the computer," said a Boston professor. "And [it's] more important than passing those doggone standardized tests, which probably are not showing what that student really knows." From the perspective of education professors, technology could help free kids and teachers from teaching and learning techniques, such as memorization, that in their view turn learning into a hated chore.

Professors of education are not totally indifferent to content. More than half (57%) say it is absolutely essential for teachers to be deeply knowledgeable about the content of the subjects they will teach. And occasionally a professor in a focus group voiced concern that prospective teachers lacked a sufficient comfort level with their subject matter. "...there is the content piece. I teach science methods, and I really do not feel that the two science courses they take prepare them, so they end up getting a job and really have to bone up on the science behind what they are going to teach," said a Boston professor.

But it is the process, not the content, of learning that most engages the passion and energy of teacher educators. If students learn how to learn, the content will follow naturally, these educators believe. A Boston professor said, "You can never teach enough content, so what I want my students to have is a passion to learn...I want them to be curious, I want them to go and find out. I want them to learn along with their students."

WHAT'S 7+5?

When it comes to encouraging children to use calculators early in their academic lives, professors of education see much to gain and little to lose, since by their definition learning to use such tools is a more critical objective. About 6 in 10 professors (57%) believe that such early use of calculators will improve children's problem-solving skills; only 38% think it will hamper their learning of basic arithmetic. As a mathematics specialist in Chicago said: "We have for so many years said to kids 'What's 7+5?' as if that was the important thing. The question we should be asking is 'Give me as many questions whose answer is 12...' Sure, I think kids should know the multiplication tables, but I wouldn't hold a kid back from doing other stuff if they didn't."

For their part, ordinary Americans and public school teachers seem far more concerned that kids be able to solve arithmetic problems by hand and produce the right answers. Overwhelmingly, they want students to memorize their multiplication tables and do math by hand first, rejecting the early use of calculators.[2]

FACILITATING LEARNING

Education professors thus define the essence of teaching to be showing students how to learn. Asked whether teachers should see themselves as facilitators of learning who enable students to learn on their own, or as conveyors of knowledge who enlighten students, professors of education opt for the former by an overwhelming 92% to 7% margin.

"Once you uncapture that spirit, that they know how to learn, that they want to learn, they can learn almost anything on their own," said a Boston professor. "I don't have to really impart a whole lot of content to them. I am there to direct them and to help them." In short, good teachers develop students who have the capacity to teach themselves.

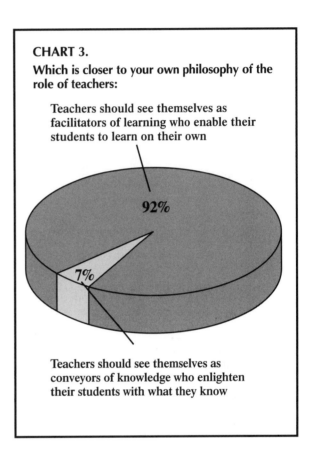

CHART 3.

Which is closer to your own philosophy of the role of teachers:

Teachers should see themselves as facilitators of learning who enable their students to learn on their own

92%

7%

Teachers should see themselves as conveyors of knowledge who enlighten their students with what they know

This view of the teacher-as-facilitator was a dominant theme in all four focus groups conducted for this study. It was never questioned or challenged, regardless of where in the country the discussions were held, whether the teacher educators worked at the college or university level, or whether they were primarily researchers or instructors. "[Teachers need] the ability to foster self-confidence in students and to develop independence of learning," said a Chicago professor. "They should see themselves not as transmitters of knowledge, but as allowing students to learn how to learn themselves." A Boston professor said, "Just like there are many ways to climb a mountain, I think it is liberating for us to teach our future teachers the variety of ways that problems can be solved, that sometimes there are no correct answers – that the process is sometimes much more important than the end result."

NO "SAGE ON THE STAGE"

Under this perspective, the learning enterprise becomes a partnership and collaboration, and not only between teacher and student, but among teachers themselves. "To be a facilitator of learning is much more difficult than being the sage on the stage," said a Los Angeles professor, "and to be effective, you need support. The support system these new teachers need . . . [so] they can network, they can talk, these kinds of things."

> "We have to think differently about how you assemble a group of caring, passionate learners. Children happen to be part of a team of learners."
> – Boston professor

Education professors report they prepare prospective teachers to teach in schools where partnership and collaboration – not isolation – are the norm. By an overwhelming margin (88% versus 11%), education professors think it is more important for their programs to prepare teachers to teach collaboratively rather than to prepare them to teach alone. A Boston professor's comment reflected this thinking: "We have to think differently about how you assemble a group of caring, passionate learners. Children happen to be part of the team of learners. Trying to load it all up on one teacher to do it all in the classroom is just not the way to think about it. It is like putting together an orchestra."

The professor's vision contrasts sharply with the experience many frontline teachers encounter once they are on the job. In earlier Public Agenda research, teachers routinely complained that teaching is an isolated and isolating experience.[3] This comment, pulled from a focus group of public school teachers, was typical: "There is no career as isolated as mine. I can go all day without talking to anyone over 21 years old. We don't see other teachers at work."

Professors of education further believe that collaboration should extend beyond school walls. They envision "communities of learning" where teachers, parents, and community members team up, share observations, pool resources, and coordinate efforts on behalf of students. "It takes a whole village to help a teacher," said a professor in Los Angeles. "If school districts don't help them, if communities don't help them, if we don't get public policy that says we value teachers . . . we can't do it alone."

Teachers of teachers want to discard what they see as crude and outdated tools of teaching and managing classrooms – techniques the public often sees as part-and-parcel of good schooling. They resist approaches that rely on competition, reward and punishment, memorization, or multiple-choice questions.

Professors of education regard teaching as an elaborate, highly evolved craft practiced by specialists trained in the latest techniques and supported by the latest research. As a consequence, they see little justification for using such "old-fashioned" methods of teaching as memorization, multiple-choice exams, competition for academic honors, and rewards for good behavior.

NO STARS FOR GOOD BEHAVIOR, NO HONOR ROLL

About half the professors of education surveyed (52%) would like to see less reliance on prizes that reward good classroom behavior. "Giving a child a reward on an occasional basis is fine," allowed a Chicago professor, "but when you have a system of doing for rewards, I react very viscerally. I don't like hearing about a kid who's high-achieving [and] doing things in the classroom for stars."

Moreover, the majority of education professors dislike academic competition as a way of motivating students to learn. Only one-third (33%) consider competition for rewards such as honor rolls a valuable incentive to foster learning, while 64% think schools should avoid competition. Some would go further and switch from grading students according to their individual effort to giving students grades for group effort. When asked to choose between two distinct ways of motivating kids to learn, 47% endorse team projects where the group shares a single grade and the team demonstrates what it learned, while 46% endorse individual projects where each student is graded individually and must personally demonstrate what he or she has learned.

MEMORIZATION: HAZARDOUS TO YOUR HEALTH?

For professors of education, perhaps the most egregious violations of their vision of learning occur when students are expected to memorize facts or take standardized exams. In focus groups, they often talked about such tools with particular disdain.

Fully 6 in 10 education professors (60%) would like to see less reliance on memorization in today's classrooms. When pressed by the focus group moderator as to whether there was really nothing that ought to be memorized, they occasionally conceded

that memorization might sometimes be appropriate. But they would immediately insist, as this Boston professor did, that memorization "has to be connected to concepts, because," he explained, "memory for its own sake is dangerous, politically dangerous. You think about when people have to memorize and spout back and you think about autocratic societies." Or, as this Chicago professor explained, even when memorizing, the *how* is more important than the *what*: "Knowing ways to memorize is very important. The thing you're memorizing in itself may not be important, but it's important to know how you can memorize things."

STANDARDIZED TESTS: SERIOUS FOLLY

Standardized tests relying on explicit right and wrong answers are seen by education professors as more serious folly. Fully 78% want less reliance on multiple-choice exams in the schools. "It's not just a base of knowledge so that they can read and know, recite and pick the right answer," insisted a Chicago professor. "They need to be able to apply that knowledge to something else."

The idea that filling in a circle could measure learning seems improbable to most education professors. They don't believe standardized tests demonstrate learning, nor are they willing to place high stakes on the results of such exams. "The fact is that all of the data say standardized tests don't predict what they are intended to. They just don't do it...There is no standardized test that is good," said a Boston professor.

> **"When you have a system of doing for rewards, I react very viscerally. I don't like hearing about a kid who's high-achieving [and] doing things in the classroom for stars." – Chicago professor**

Just as they were almost contemptuous of multiple-choice tests, some professors of education could not easily bring themselves to answer the closed-ended questions in this study. The notion that they would be forced to commit to one word or one choice that summarized their views – without the possibility of explanation and elaboration – was unpalatable. Public Agenda staff fielded an unusually high number of calls from respondents who wanted to elaborate on their views, or explain why they could not, in good conscience, participate in the survey.

JUST FILLING OUT BUBBLES

In sharp contrast to multiple-choice tests, education professors embrace portfolios as a vehicle that allows students to demonstrate what they have absorbed and learned. "It shows you know by doing it, not filling out bubbles," said a Los Angeles professor. "Authentic assessment provides a way to see different ways of knowing, more ways of solving problems … [but] parents and politicians like scores, because they're simple." Nearly 8 in 10 professors (78%) call for more reliance on portfolios and other authentic assessments. A New York professor said, "I'd like to go with performance-based assessment as the most important catalyst for change, to move away from standard answers or the one right answer – for children to display, perform, demonstrate what they know."

> **"The research shifts and people take a more extreme position than they need to…and then you get polarization."**
> **– Los Angeles professor**

BACKED BY RESEARCH?

In the focus groups, education professors often explained their preferred teaching methods by referring to research that supports their methods. Many expressed disappointment and some exasperation that so much current educational research seems to be ignored or dismissed by the public. But other comments suggested that acceptance of the current body of research is not monolithic, nor are professors always pleased by how research is utilized in "real life." In Los Angeles, one professor who was clearly an inside critic of his field voiced serious doubt about the rigor of education research – and its politicization: "The problem with a lot of the research is that it creates cults," he said. "Education is a profession that brings in a lot of people who think they know what is going on…Research on learning styles, for instance, is very flawed."

Interestingly, his observation led another professor to comment on the whole-language issue that has generated so much controversy, especially in California. The research, he said, was often subject to political spin-control: "The research shifts and people take a more extreme position than they need to or believe in to counterbalance something else, and then you get polarization. That's not really appropriate. We've gone through this with whole reading and Ebonics."

Professors of education hold a vision of public education that seems fundamentally at odds with that of public school teachers, students, and the public. While the public's priorities are discipline, basic skills, and good behavior in the classroom, teachers of teachers severely downplay such goals.

THE PUBLIC'S PRIORITIES

Ordinary Americans, along with teachers and students, have made their essential expectations of public education abundantly clear: safe, orderly schools that graduate students who master basic skills, develop good work habits, and learn such values as honesty and respect. Each group may express a slightly different ordering of priorities and criticisms, but the commonalities are striking. Moreover, these themes emerge across different segments of the population – parents or non-parents; whites, African-Americans, or Hispanics; and different states or districts. To be sure, this "mission list" is not the sum total of the public's expectations, but it captures its minimum requirements.

Like ordinary citizens, public school teachers place a premium on discipline and order at school, sometimes supporting measures to achieve these goals by majorities even larger than those of the general public. For example, nearly 9 in 10 teachers (88%) favor removing persistent troublemakers from class; and roughly the same percentage favor emphasizing work habits such as being on time, dependability, and discipline.[4] Even students complain about classrooms where disorder often reigns. About 7 in 10 students say that too many disruptive students are a serious problem in their school; another 7 in 10 (68%) point to cheating as a serious problem; and half complain that too many students get away with being late to class and not doing their school work.[5]

Not only do ordinary Americans prize these "non-negotiable" objectives with resolute intensity, but many also are alarmed that the public schools fail to achieve them. Sixty percent of Americans surveyed say their public schools do not place enough emphasis on the basics such as reading, writing, and math. Slightly over half (52%) say their schools don't teach good work habits, while another 54% are not satisfied with how teachers deal with discipline in their classrooms.[6] Nearly half say a high school diploma is no guarantee that the typical student has learned the basics.[7]

STRIKINGLY DIFFERENT VIEWS

But ask the professors of education – the teachers of teachers – what they seek to transmit to their student teachers, and a very different agenda emerges. When asked how essential it is to impart to future teachers a series of qualities – ranging from lifelong learning to theories of child development to maintaining order in the classroom – education professors put the public's priorities squarely at the bottom of their list. Only 12% consider it "absolutely essential" for teachers to expect students to be neat, on time, and polite. Only 19% believe it is "absolutely essential" for graduates of education programs to stress correct spelling, grammar, and punctuation in their teaching. Slightly more than one-third (37%) say it is absolutely essential to develop teachers trained to maintain discipline and order in the classroom.

Of the 40 education professors interviewed in the focus groups, only two spoke about the importance of discipline and order in the classroom. One of the two, a Chicago professor, said, "I believe discipline is a prerequisite to teaching, and our [teacher-] students have to be taught how to control classes." His peers responded with a telling silence.

> **Seventy-nine percent of these teachers of teachers say "the general public has outmoded and mistaken beliefs about what good teaching means."**

IDEAL TEACHERS

Students naturally have strong feelings on the question of what makes an effective teacher, and some items on their list of key qualities would resonate with education professors. Broad majorities of high school students – near or above 70% – say that good teachers make lessons fun and interesting, are enthusiastic and excited about their subject, and rely on hands-on projects and class discussions. But if education professors were to ask high school students to grade teachers on attaining such qualities, the reports they would receive would not be comforting. Students make it clear that such teachers are not commonplace: Fewer than 30% say most of their teachers display each of those qualities.[8]

What's more, high school students say they learn well in a school environment in which teachers are stricter and more directive than education professors suggest. Almost 8 in 10 teens (79%) say most students would learn more if their schools routinely assured that kids were on time and completed their homework.[9] Six in 10 (61%) say having their class work checked regularly and being forced to redo it until it is correct would get them to learn a lot more.[10] When interviewed in focus groups, teens often remembered "tough" teachers with fondness: "I had a math teacher [who] was like a drill sergeant. She was nice but she was really strict. Now I don't have her this year, and looking back, I learned so much."

A QUESTION OF EMPHASIS?

A closer look does suggest some common ground between education professors and the public. Nine in 10 members of the public want schools to put more emphasis on making learning enjoyable and interesting to students.[11] The public also mildly endorses using essays or portfolios instead of multiple-choice tests (54%), as do some public school teachers (47%).[12]

> **Education professors believe that without active, engaged learning in the classroom, discipline will probably be a problem; the public, teachers, and students think that orderly classrooms are a prerequisite that must be in place before learning can take place.**

And for their part, education professors are not totally inattentive to the discipline issue. While only 37% believe discipline is "absolutely essential" (a score of 5, on a 1-to-5 scale), an additional 38% give it a rating of 4. So perhaps the gap is a function of emphasis and salience. Or perhaps it is a result of different assumptions and starting points: Education professors believe that without active, engaged learning in the classroom, discipline will probably be a problem; the public, teachers, and students think that orderly classrooms are a prerequisite that must be in place before learning can take place.

WRONG THEORIES

Interestingly, professors of education are often quite aware that the public is focused on priorities different from their own. But they are not fazed by this gap, believing that the public is not up-to-date on findings from research or especially competent to judge good schooling. In fact, 79% of these teachers of teachers say "the general public has outmoded and mistaken beliefs about what good teaching means." "The public is still thinking about teaching in the context of the factory model," said a New York professor. "There's a subject, there's a skill, you teach it to them, and they get it. That's not really the way we're learning that kids learn, nor is it the way that teachers learn."

A colleague extended the discussion to a concrete example: teaching grammar. "Some people out there may be convinced that they learned to write through rote grammar instruction, when in fact research suggests that is not the case. The public," he concluded, "carries these wrong theories about what's going on." In Los Angeles, an education professor's comments reflected the same frustration: "One of the problems that teachers face is public perception of what is the right thing to do and what isn't. Parents come from, 'We need to learn facts,' but my contention is we need to learn how to learn. I want to teach children to know how to independently learn things, and parents disagree."

COMMUNICATING WITH PARENTS

Only 27% of the education professors surveyed report that they or their programs place great emphasis on teaching prospective teachers how to communicate with parents. But even when education professors do talk about improving communication and increasing parental involvement in the schools, they have a very distinct picture in mind. In New York, for example, communicating with parents was deemed important because parents needed to be "brought up to speed," to be educated or reeducated about how learning ought to happen in today's classroom.

"We're seeing the need to make more crucial, reflective alliances with parents," said a professor. "There's never much talk about the processes of teaching in public school. So people will carry away stories about public education that don't really fit with what happened ... And nothing's going to change unless we bring the public in when they have their kids in school and say, 'Look, this is what we're doing.'"

But other respondents voiced a different kind of wish – that the public simply stay out of the education business: "What bothers me is for the public to make the decision of what I, the teacher, should do in the classroom. I really resent that," complained a Los Angeles professor. "They're getting into methodology, and what methodology [you can teach] they're going to tell you by law."

Even as they advocate an ambitious teaching agenda, education professors harbor serious doubts about whether they are adequately preparing teachers to succeed in the real world. Most education professors have been out of the classroom for many years and they themselves suspect they are too detached from today's schools. Most also have concerns about the quality of prospective teachers in their programs.

TRAPPED IN THE IVORY TOWER

Education professors have, by their own report, set an ambitious educational agenda, but they also express serious doubts about whether they, their programs, and their students are up to the task.

Education professors worry, for example, that they may be too distant from the daily realities of the public schools. More than 8 in 10 (84%) believe most professors of education should spend more time in the K-12 classroom. Many suspect their detachment from the public school classrooms harms their ability to prepare prospective teachers for the challenges they will face. "I really have to make an effort to get out into the schools sometimes," confessed a Boston professor. "I get trapped in the ivory tower. And I don't like that. It would be better for me if we had better partnerships between schools and universities."

> "I really have to make an effort to get out into the schools sometimes. I get trapped in the ivory tower. And I don't like that." – Boston professor

Some also doubt that the teaching techniques they model with the prospective teachers enrolled in their programs will actually work with young kids, who are in school because they have to be. "I have 25 or 30 [teacher-] students in the classroom who are there willingly, paying good money," pointed out a Chicago professor. "And they can't think, 'I'm going to take these great techniques that I love as a student, and I'm going to be able to do that with sixth graders.' You have a whole different agenda in a sixth grade classroom. My using those techniques doesn't really show them anything except that it works with college students. They really need to see other people who are teaching sixth graders."

CLASSROOM EXPERIENCE . . . LONG AGO

There are compelling indications that education professors have reason to be concerned about being detached from the K-12 classrooms and the day-to-day responsibilities of frontline teachers. Seventeen percent of those surveyed report that they have never been a K-12 classroom teacher. The experience of those who had been K-12 teachers is perhaps more striking: About half (51%) say it has been more than 15 years since they were in that position. A recent *New York Times* article about the closing of the University of Chicago's School of Education linked that situation to a disconnect with "day-to-day involvement with teacher training and schools" and a growing focus on the purely theoretical aspects of education.[13]

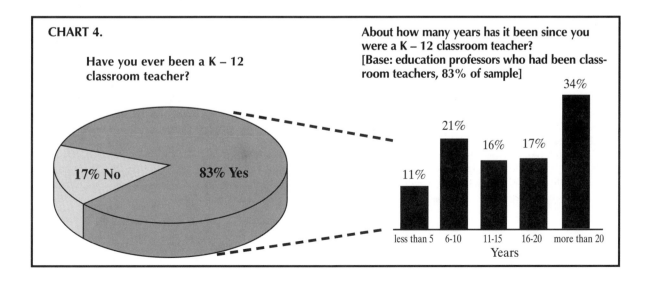

CHART 4.

Have you ever been a K – 12 classroom teacher?

17% No   83% Yes

About how many years has it been since you were a K – 12 classroom teacher?
[Base: education professors who had been classroom teachers, 83% of sample]

less than 5	6-10	11-15	16-20	more than 20
11%	21%	16%	17%	34%

Years

Moreover, education professors report there is little incentive or capacity in the higher education system to steer them into K-12 classrooms to practice what they preach. While talking about time he had spent in classrooms, a Chicago professor admitted, "It doesn't happen too much, but it should." But he explained, "There's no mechanism to do it. They don't know how to pay us, we're on different pension systems. We have different licenses, there's liability insurance. It's very complex." Other education professors pointed out that the demands they face – the "publish or perish" requirement, their supervisory obligations, and their teaching duties – make anything more than brief school visits impractical.

A LOW-STATUS PROFESSION

The doubts education professors acknowledge about themselves often extend to their student body, the prospective teachers they train. "Historically," said a Chicago professor, "teaching was dominated by women, and it was considered a low-status thing to do . . . there's a joke that there are three reasons to go into teaching: June, July, and August. Sometimes we get students who are picking teaching as a career for the wrong reasons."

Three out of every 4 education professors (75%) complain that too many of their students have trouble writing essays that are free of mistakes in grammar and spelling.

Fully 7 in 10 professors of education (72%) say they often or sometimes come across students they seriously doubt have what it takes to be a teacher. In the Los Angeles focus group, much of the talk concerned the class-size reduction law now in effect in California, a law which has created an enormous demand for new teachers. Several participants worried about the quality of people entering their programs in response to that need, feeling that many new entrants lacked the passion or skills needed to be good teachers.

"There are a lot of people who don't fit our idea of the good teacher coming in," said one professor. "There are teachers in classrooms with contracts, and my gut feeling is they're not qualified. They're not academically qualified; they don't have the class-room management techniques." Another said, "You can only do so much with current material; we need to emphasize growing teachers at lower levels. And it's going to take a while."

WEEDING OUT UNSUITABLE TEACHERS

Education professors report some tell-tale indicators that their student body is far from ideal. The very same issue that troubles the public – too many kids graduating without the basic skills – troubles education professors about the prospective teachers they teach. Three out of every 4 education professors (75%) complain that too many of their students have trouble writing essays free of mistakes in grammar and spelling. A Chicago professor talked about her response to prospective teachers who have writing problems: "I really try to refer them to places where they can get help . . . I also refer them to grammar books. This is a constant battle for me and these students because they say to me, 'This is not an English class, that's not what you're supposed to be doing.'"

Only 4% of education professors report that their programs typically dismiss students considered unsuitable for teaching. Most (67%) say these students are counseled to reconsider their career choice, while another 20% say such students are referred to remediation.

Ultimately, an overwhelming majority – 86% – admit they need to do a better job of dismissing unsuitable teachers. "I think we have to do a better job of the weeding-out process," volunteered a Boston professor. "Not everybody who enters my college who thinks they should be a teacher should be a teacher. We have to be more hard-nosed about who that person is."

A few seem reconciled to some mediocrity, seeing it as the inevitable result of having to prepare so many teachers. "We're aware that our profession attracts students who are at the less capable end of the academic scale," one Chicago professor stated. "But so what? We have 30-some thousand teachers in Chicago. Does anyone think they're all geniuses? Give me a break!"

TEST THE TEACHERS

When asked to identify the biggest challenge facing teacher education programs, the recruitment of quality teachers was named by more professors (24%) than any other factor. And in what is perhaps an indication of their concern about teacher quality, 67% of the education professors surveyed endorse without reservation a proposal to require teachers to pass tests demonstrating proficiency in key subjects before they are hired.

18   © 1997 Public Agenda

Almost as many (63%) frankly admit that education programs often fail to prepare teachers for the challenges of teaching in the real world. "I heard the latest figure is that within 5 years half the people who started out teaching are no longer teaching," said a Chicago education professor. Yet an overwhelming majority remain convinced that the students their own programs produce are ready to succeed. Nearly 7 in 10 (68%) say that most prospective teachers who graduate from their program come close to their ideal vision of the classroom teacher, suggesting that perhaps their doubts center on teachers graduating from other institutions' programs.

> **"You can only do so much with current material; we need to emphasize growing teachers at lower levels. And it's going to take a while."**
> **– Los Angeles professor**

FOLLOWING MY HEART

A natural question is whether the doubts they themselves admit to – their concerns about the quality of the teacher pool, their fears that they are detached from real classrooms, and their fears that prospective teachers are not prepared for the real world – lead education professors to reexamine their idealized and elaborate teaching agenda. In focus groups, the moderator asked if their doubts suggest the pursuit of goals more in tune with reality. In other words, are they letting the perfect be the enemy of the good?

The response was almost instinctive resistance and recoil. In the words of one Chicago professor, "If we weren't the idealists, who is going to be?" In Los Angeles, a professor said, "It's my obligation as a teacher trainer to follow my heart, and I don't think the expectations can ever be too great, because we're talking about our future. It may sound idealistic, but that's what keeps me going as a teacher."

Education professors support a core curriculum and higher academic standards but often balk at requiring students to pass tests that demonstrate relatively simple academic skills and knowledge.

YES TO STANDARDS – AT LEAST IN CONCEPT

Perhaps the most influential reform working its way across the nation's education systems is the standards movement – an effort to specify the skills and knowledge youngsters ought to know, measure whether they've mastered them, and hold schools, students, and others accountable for what is learned.

The public evinces very strong support for higher academic standards, motivated in large part by an attempt to guarantee that high school graduates have a grasp of basic academic skills and knowledge. To the public, demonstrating the basics is an absolutely essential starting point, and many Americans – nearly half – suspect that a high school diploma today fails to guarantee that "standard."[14] Thus, the public follows its support for higher standards with support for school policies that impose consequences and academic sanctions if students fail to achieve the standards.

Education professors also support such standards, at least on a conceptual level. Two-thirds (66%) say today's public schools expect too little of their students when it comes to academic achievement. Seventy-two percent consider it absolutely essential for prospective teachers to have high expectations of all students. Seventy-one percent believe that setting up clear guidelines on what kids should learn and teachers should teach in every major subject will improve education. "The national standards in science education are going to do a lot; I'm putting a lot into that," said a New York professor.

> **Only 55% would require kids to demonstrate they know proper spelling, grammar, and punctuation before getting a diploma.**

Education professors expect higher academic standards to produce positive results. Two-thirds (66%) say kids would pay more attention and study harder if the public schools adopted higher standards. Seven in 10 (70%) say kids would actually learn more as a result. Many also believe there will be costs associated with this reform, with almost half (47%) predicting that more kids will drop out. Another 27% say that as a result of higher academic expectations more students will dislike education and resist learning.

RELUCTANT TO TEST

But while supporting standards in concept, professors of education seem reluctant to put into place concrete, high-stakes tests that would signal when kids are meeting the standards or at least heading in the right direction.

Raising the bar of academic requirements for younger children garners only tepid support from education professors. Six in ten (60%) do support what standards advocates regard as crucial – requiring kids to pass tests demonstrating proficiency in key subjects before they can graduate. But only 49% believe raising the standards of promotion from grade school to junior high and letting kids move ahead only when they pass a test showing they've reached those standards, would do a great deal to improve academic achievement. In sharp contrast, the percentage reaches 70% among the general public.[15]

And while 76% of education professors would not allow kids to graduate from high school unless they clearly demonstrate they can write and speak English well, many balk at requiring kids to demonstrate specific language skills. Only 55% would require kids to demonstrate they know proper spelling, grammar, and punctuation before getting a diploma.

Education professors show similar discomfort with another test of common knowledge: Just 33% would require kids to know the names and geographic location of the 50 states before getting a diploma. "Why should they know that?" asked a Los Angeles professor. "They need to know how to find out where they are. When I need to know that, I can go look it up. That's the important piece, and here is what's hard to get parents to understand."

EXPLAINING THE GAP

On the one hand, education professors support the concept of higher academic standards and expectations; on the other, they seem reluctant to place tangible stakes on their achievement – to put teeth in the standards. What accounts for the gap?

For one thing, as we have seen, professors of education question the reliability and value of standardized tests – generally a major component of initiatives to raise standards. What's more, many professors of education believe that public concerns over the basics are wildly overblown, and that schools have the basics well in hand. Said a Boston professor, "It makes good press to say that students graduate and can't read and can't write, but 90% [sic] of the students who graduate can." The pursuit of guaranteeing the basics may seem too modest a goal to these teachers of teachers. Yet it is interesting to recall that 75% of education professors themselves complain about too many education students having "trouble writing essays free of mistakes in grammar and spelling."

Another reason teacher educators resist concrete testing for standards is a concern that it would refocus the energy in classrooms on the tests and away from their definition of good teaching practices. "Helping people respond to standards is a good thing," remarked a New York professor, who also issued a warning about such standards: "If they're not adhered to or achieved in the right way, they stifle creativity. I know this from talking to students in secondary education. I say, 'Try this innovative approach, try to get the students to do a little cooperative learning.' They say, 'No, the teacher's got to get this in through the Regents [standardized exams New York high schoolers take for their diploma] and we've got to get this done because we have to reach this standard that the state has imposed.'"

> "Standards is nothing to get real excited about. They put a lot of money into it. It is somebody's quick and dirty solution to a very complicated problem."
> – Boston professor

MANY VARIATIONS

And perhaps because professors of education have thought long and hard about many of these issues, their views are often nuanced and complex. In the focus group discussions, the education professors were often equivocal about any reform proposal: hedging, specifying conditions, and requiring elaborations. It is far easier, therefore, to gain their assent to broad conceptual proposals than to concrete ones, to which all sorts of exceptions and conditions pop up in their minds. A New York professor tried to explain her hesitancy about standards this way: "When you say *what* students should learn I think we would all agree on certain concepts, ideas, experiences that all students should have in common. But when you say *when* they should learn, and *how* they should learn, then there are many variations."

Nor is it uncommon to find education professors supporting goals for the schools but declining to make them a concrete part of their own teaching

agenda. They support, for example, having schools emphasize "such work habits as being on time, dependable, and disciplined" by a wide margin (78%). But, as seen earlier, only 12% believe it is absolutely essential for public school teachers to expect students to be neat, on time, and polite.

SUBJECT TO ABUSE

Moreover, since education professors do not believe academic sanctions are an important part of motivating kids to learn, high-stakes exams that would hold back under-performing kids strike them as counterproductive and subject to abuse. A New York professor said, "Standards can sometimes be used to punish individuals, in particular the disabled population, who are going to be thrown into this pool...[it] becomes a hammer to hit those people who did not make it. And that is not what you want education to be about."

In the end, there is considerable doubt among education professors that higher standards – and what comes with them – are a cure for what ails the schools. When standards and discipline are matched up against more resources, smaller classes, and increased support as the "best way to improve the schools," two-thirds (68%) favor investing in resources while only 29% favor higher standards and more discipline. "Standards is nothing to get real excited about," said a Boston professor. "They put a lot of money into it. It is somebody's quick and dirty solution to a very complicated problem."

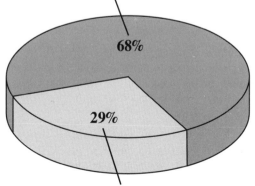

CHART 5.

Best way to improve local public schools:

Give them more money for up-to-date equipment, smaller classes, and increased support for kids with the greatest problems

68%

29%

Have higher standards and more discipline – things that do not require additional money

SAYING AMEN TO HIRSCH?

Ideological firefights over teaching courses in Western civilization or the classical works that constitute "the canon" routinely break out in America's universities, spilling over into academic journals and the political arena. The tone of these conflicts suggests a veritable war, pitting those who assail "dead, white European males" on one side against the defenders of the pillars of civilization on the other.

It is somewhat surprising, therefore, that education professors seem generally comfortable with relying upon a Western civilization-based core curriculum in the public schools. Six in 10 (59%) would approve of a core curriculum with specific knowledge and skill standards spelled out for each grade level. And their responses to questions about whether "the public schools must teach a core body of knowledge that includes great literature, such as Shakespeare, and important historical documents such as the Constitution" – questions intended to capture the pro- and anti-canon sentiment in the core curriculum debate – place most education professors squarely in the pro-Western civilization camp. For example, 3 in 4 (77%) say it is critical for students to "gain a shared understanding of this body of knowledge because it has defined our culture." Another 3 in 4 (76%) say that "any student who receives a high school diploma without being exposed to this core body of knowledge has been cheated in a fundamental way."

> **"I'd rather they understand the concept of colonialism and imperialism than to know when Columbus discovered America."**
> **– New York professor**

A 'RELATIVIST' CONTINGENT

Survey and focus group responses did uncover a significant "relativist" contingent which finds it inappropriate to promulgate the canon in the public schools. For example, 37% say "designating a core body of knowledge amounts to unfairly imposing one group's cultural values on others." "I'd rather they understand the concept of colonialism and imperialism," said a New York professor, "than to know when Columbus discovered America."

About one-third (34%) say a core curriculum "would needlessly distract teachers from teaching kids how to learn." Finally, 3 in 10 (30%) argue that "since there is no consensus on what constitutes this core body of knowledge, teachers cannot be expected to teach it." A Chicago professor said, "When I read [E. D.] Hirsch's book *Cultural Literacy*, I don't find myself opposed to people knowing those things... [but] I find Hirsch and myself to be keyed into a particular culture, a particular ethnicity... And I don't want to impose mine on people whose culture is different."

TEACHING KIDS TO HATE IT

If most education professors believe that a student who has not been exposed to the Western canon (Shakespeare included) has been "cheated," one might also expect many to support a requirement that kids know classic works from such writers as Shakespeare and Plato before receiving a diploma. But only 16% of all professors surveyed do so. What explains the drop-off?

Support for the Western canon comes with some qualifications and caveats borne of the same thinking that drives professors to support standards more in concept than in practice. "You think of Shakespeare as something that should obviously be on the list," began a New York professor, "but more people have been destroyed in their connection with Shakespeare because of inappropriate teaching at an inappropriate level. Something that looks terrific in the canon – like in literature – we wind up teaching kids to hate. If they hate it, what's the point?"

A Chicago professor voiced these reservations: "With the core curriculum, we forget that these ought to be ongoing conversations that never end. Unfortunately, what happens is that people engage in these activities thinking that there's an end, that we're going to come up with a list or test, as opposed to teachers constantly haggling back and forth."

Professors of education consistently resist initiatives that in their view would remove the mystery and discovery from teaching and learning by codifying and enforcing a particular body of knowledge. Settling on a required academic agenda, many believe, would lead to mindless teaching and parroted learning, undermining a vision of education based on constant questioning. Said a Chicago professor, "I have yet to see anything in Hirsch that I wouldn't want my students to know, but I wouldn't say 'this is it,' nor would I say that if they failed to achieve it, they failed in their education. Education to me is a process, not a product. Common knowledge is a product."

THE CONSERVATIVE – LIBERAL SPLIT

But even as the clash over a core curriculum seems unexpectedly muted, a closer look reveals powerful ideological differences on many issues, signaling that some of the harshest battles in this realm of academia may indeed be driven by conservative - liberal disagreements.

As part of the study, professors were asked to state their political leanings, and the study results show conservative (15%) and liberal (29%) education professors often disagree over the goals and methods of teaching. While more than half of conservatives (54%) believe academic sanctions are an important way to motivate kids to learn, only 31% of liberals agree. Conservatives are far more likely than liberals to support a requirement that kids know proper spelling, grammar, and punctuation before they graduate high school (68% to 42%).

Conservatives are also more likely than liberals to worry that the early use of calculators in elementary schools can hamper kids from learning basic arithmetic skills (50% to 31%). And when it comes to students who are new immigrants, 82% of conservatives – but only 44% of liberals – believe the schools' priority should be to help them learn America's language and culture as quickly as possible, even if their native language and culture suffer as a result. Education professors often cite research when justifying their preferred pedagogical practices, but this study suggests that it may be their self-ascribed ideological loyalties that seem to partially explain their preferences.

THE MIDDLE GROUND

These percentage differences are sizable and occur repeatedly throughout the study. These differences might lead one to conclude that the teacher education field is indeed extremely polarized. Although this is sometimes the case, liberal and conservative professors agree on many issues. For example, conservatives (86%) and liberals (92%) both believe teachers should see themselves as facilitators of learning, not as conveyors of knowledge. Another example: Only 19% of conservatives and only 15% of liberals believe in requiring kids to know classic works from Shakespeare and Plato before graduating.

> **It is also important to keep in mind that 51% of education professors describe themselves as moderates when it comes to their political views.**

It is also important to keep in mind that 51% of education professors actually describe themselves as moderates when it comes to their political views. As one might expect, as a group, education professors who are moderates often stake a middle ground between their liberal and conservative peers.

CHART 6.

When it comes to students who are new immigrants, the public schools' primary goal should be to help new immigrants:

	Total	Conservatives	Moderates	Liberals
Absorb America's language and culture as quickly as possible, even if their native language and culture are neglected	57%	82%	59%	44%
Maintain their own language and culture, even if it takes them longer to absorb America's language and culture	40%	16%	39%	52%

Teachers of teachers think of public education as an almost sacred democratic institution that is under siege and unfairly blamed for problems not of its making. They rally to its defense and reject reforms that challenge the primacy of public schools. Education professors also believe that their own programs are unfairly blamed and unappreciated.

THE LAST PUBLIC SPACE

To professors of education, America's public school system is a critical – perhaps *the* critical – national institution, not merely because of the learning it fosters but because of the crucial democratic and social functions it serves. Virtually all of those surveyed (95%) say that the statement "public education is the nation's most critical democratic institution and should be protected at all costs" comes close to their own view; 75% say this statement comes *very* close to their views.

In the minds of education professors, public education serves a broad civic function by creating citizens capable of participating in democratic political life, regardless of their cultural origins. In the words of a New York professor, "I really feel that public schools are one of our last public spaces. And it is really a part of our democratic society...this is the way all of this diversity can be put together."

Education professors also believe that public education's mission is to redress some of the inequities borne of poverty and the nation's social problems, to level the playing field so that kids have a chance for a better life in spite of tough beginnings. "It is important to remember that public schools are the last public institution where society is working with every youngster and working out its social ills," reflected a Boston professor.

HELP FOR THOSE WHO NEED IT MOST

To further this vision, education professors make a major investment in training prospective teachers to work in classrooms where diversity and differences are the norm. More than half (54%) say that their programs place "a lot" of emphasis on preparing prospective teachers to teach kids from diverse ethnic and cultural backgrounds. "The one concept I want my students to have firmly within them is that they will be always struggling to provide their students equal educational opportunities [EEO]," said a Los Angeles professor. "You're never going to reach EEO, but the more you try to provide it the better. In the past, we have not strived the same for everybody. I want my students committed and to understand that the strategies you're going to use are different from Mary Brown to Juanita Jimenez."

Teacher educators seem especially intent on insuring that students who might have been neglected or overlooked in the past will now benefit from new teachers who are sensitive and alert to their needs. About 4 in 10 (43%) say their programs place "a lot" of emphasis on training prospective teachers to identify learning disabled students.

> "I really feel that public schools are one of our last public spaces. And it is really a part of our democratic society...this is the way all of this diversity can be put together."
> – New York professor

There is one group of students – those considered academically gifted – whose needs appear to carry less priority than other groups. Teacher education programs seem to invest far less energy in training prospective teachers to identify talented and gifted students in their classrooms; in fact, only 15% put "a lot" of emphasis on identifying such students. One professor in Los Angeles explained this as simply recognizing who needed less help. "The conventional wisdom," he said, "is that they can take care of themselves."

But another professor had an even broader explanation for the relatively mild interest in training prospective teachers to identify gifted kids: "It's a fundamental philosophical issue...If education is the major building block of a democratic society, then you worry more about raising the floor...the fundamental goal is to give as many children as possible the tools to participate in a democratic society." And while schools in the past would often track students by ability, the strategy has apparently fallen into disfavor with many educators. A little over half of the education professors surveyed (54%) favor less reliance on homogenous grouping; and an identical 54% majority believes that mixing fast and slow learners in the same class would improve kids' academic achievement.

DEFENDING PUBLIC SCHOOLS

The sense that the public school system is the nation's cornerstone democratic institution may explain why education professors strongly resist proposals to offer parents vouchers, something they fear would undermine the institution they so prize. Given a list of seven measures designed to capture popular reform proposals currently "in the air" – from smaller schools, to public school choice, to teacher testing, to vouchers – vouchers garner the lowest support and most resistance from teacher educators. A plurality (44%) disapproves of vouchers, and an additional 37% would approve of them only under certain conditions. "A lot of rhetoric on vouchers is rampant individualism," said a New York professor, "and forgets the fact that we are in a society together, and we depend on each other."

Many education professors do endorse providing more choice for parents as long as choice is permitted only within the public school domain. A 52% majority approves of allowing parents to choose among public schools; only 12% would disapprove of the measure.

Not surprisingly, political views strongly affect attitudes on how to improve the public schools. Liberals overwhelmingly (67%) believe that one of the most effective ways to improve the schools is to give them a lot more money; few conservatives – only 31% – concur. Given two strategies for improving the public schools – more money and equipment versus higher standards and more discipline – conservative professors are far more likely than their liberal colleagues to opt for standards and discipline (59% to 20%). Liberal professors are far more likely to opt for money and equipment (77% to 40%).

Conservatives are more likely to tout school choice and free-market proposals. Two-thirds (66%) of conservatives endorse, without conditions, public school choice – while only 44% of liberals do the same. And conservatives are four times more likely than liberals to endorse vouchers without conditions (40% to 10%). While 67% of conservatives believe teacher tenure is often an obstacle to school improvement, only 43% of liberals agree.

EVEN IN THE WORST CASE

To gauge how committed education professors are to public education, the survey presented them with this scenario: A public school district in a low-income community has failed to give kids a quality education for 15 years – even after it received additional resources and new leadership. Which of four options – charter schools, more time and money, a state takeover, or private school vouchers – would they want to try next? Even in this worst-case scenario, only 19% would "give parents vouchers to make private schools a more affordable choice." This is virtually indistinguishable from the 21% who would give the same district still more time and money to improve. The plurality (40%) would opt for strongly encouraging the creation of charter schools in the district.

> "A lot of rhetoric on vouchers is rampant individualism and forgets the fact that we are in a society together, and we depend on each other."
> – New York professor

One might think that charter schools could be a preferred reform since they can work within the public school model. But in response to another question on charter schools, only 40% approve of them without reservation, while an additional 47% would approve but only under certain conditions. The reservations are at least partly driven by suspicions that charter schools siphon off resources from the public schools. A Boston professor said, "I think a lot of these things sound good on paper, but in reality tend to undermine the existing public school system...I use as an example charter schools. I think on paper they look wonderful, they give you all kinds of opportunities, until you really look at them closely. And essentially they are pulling [out] tax money that is supporting the public school. All of these things are just filtering off from what should be our strongest asset in this country."

There is a corresponding resentment of private schools and a sense that they are wrongly used as the standard against which to compare public schools. Two-thirds of the teachers of teachers (67%) believe that when "you take into account the differences in the children they teach," private schools are not better than public schools. The focus group discussions sometimes revealed suspicions that private schools flourish for reasons other than academic achievement. "I think parochial schools are a blatant example of white flight," said a Boston professor. "I don't think people are in them for religious reasons... They are there because they are all-white schools."

A PERSONAL STRUGGLE

Some professors had faced the decision of where to send their own children, and their comments indicated that this provided an emotional litmus test of sorts. "I actually did what all the choice advocates describe," said one New York professor. "I was a middle-class parent who said, 'I will seek out the location where I can respect and have confidence in the public schools.' And I am a public school advocate. But if I had stayed in the city, I would have almost definitely sent my child to private school. I made the choice to move to another district in order to send my child to a public school."

> "If I had stayed in the city, I would have almost definitely sent my child to private school. I made the choice to move to another district in order to send my child to a public school." – New York professor

About one-quarter (26%) of those professors with children have sent their children, at least at some point, to private school. And one-third (34%) of the educators whose kids attended only public school admitted they had seriously considered sending their children to private school instead. Such calculations and actions often led to intense internal struggling.

"For me, it's a moral issue," said another New York professor. "Particularly as an educator, you think, 'What am I doing, pulling my kids out of a school where I could exert pressure for change?' But then when you look at it from your child's perspective, you say, 'Do I sacrifice my child?'"

POLITICALLY MOTIVATED?

The educators' sense of the public schools as a fundamental cornerstone of democratic society is coupled with a sense that public schools are now under severe stress, pressed by too many social problems and vulnerable to politically-motivated criticisms and negative press coverage. More than 8 in 10 (85%) say that "the schools are expected to deal with too many social problems." In discussing the difficulties of teaching, one university professor in Boston said, "The task of [teaching] is exacerbated by the ills of society that are put upon the schools. The school is asked to solve far, far too many problems...[Yet] we must, as a society, do something for this generation of kids."

As for the doubts the public displays, professors of education believe these are driven by negative media stories – either a lack of information or a glut of misinformation. Two-thirds (65%) say the "decline in public confidence in public schools is a result of negative press coverage." And more than half (54%) suspect some of the criticisms are politically motivated and "come from right-wing groups who want to undermine public education." A New York professor's focus group comment illustrates this thinking: "I think we have to be careful about media portrayal of schools...It's often extremely negative, and a lot of that has to do with political motivations to essentially shut down what is the last public space to prepare citizens."

In the face of such obstacles and challenges, many professors think the schools deserve praise. Most give the public schools high marks, with 76% saying the schools they have personally come in contact with are doing an excellent or good job.

THE EMBATTLED TEACHER PROGRAMS

Just as they feel the public schools are under siege, professors of education believe their own profession is not given the respect it deserves and that teacher education programs are often unfairly maligned.

Fully 82% say teacher education programs are unfairly blamed for the problems facing public education. "The major reason I was attracted to this [focus group] conversation," said a New York professor, "was that for once, teacher educators were going to have something to say about what's going on in the schools. Usually when all the blame is laid out, it falls at the door of the teacher educators."

There is a widespread sense among education professors that their stature is questioned even in the halls of academia. Roughly 8 in 10 (79%) say that teacher education programs are often treated as second-class citizens within the higher education system. "Not enough money, not enough people, not enough grants are available to us," complained a Chicago professor. And to add insult to injury, many professors of education (54%) also believe that "education programs are too often seen as cash cows by university administrators."

PEOPLE THINK ANYONE CAN DO IT

To many teacher educators, the existence of alternative teacher certification programs is a signal that the value of their programs is doubted. Over half (56%) say such programs weaken the overall quality of teachers while 37% instead say they are "a much needed solution to the shortage of public school teachers."

Some were open to the possibility that alternative certification programs would tap needed talent. "I think there are good teachers that come out of that system," said another professor in the same focus group, "and I do believe there should be some alternative certification... there are people who are just naturals and they don't need all our pedagogy." But others were openly disdainful. "People think anyone can do it," said a Chicago professor, "because they watch us all day long. That is the real problem. Everybody thinks that all they have to do is get up there and open their mouth."

> **"People think anyone can do it... That is the real problem. Everybody thinks that all they have to do is get up there and open their mouth."**
> **– Chicago professor**

INSPIRED, BUT POORLY ARMED
By Deborah Wadsworth

Idealists can often light the way as humanity strives to improve itself, but is there a point when a visionary agenda is so detached from daily concerns that it becomes counterproductive? Professors of education have a particular vision of what teaching should be – one that has some appealing features. But their prescriptions for the public schools gloss over the concerns voiced variously by the public, parents, classroom teachers, business leaders, education reformers, and even students themselves. This idealism might seem to be a kind of rarified blindness to many Americans – one that glorifies the ideal, quite ignoring the possible or the useful. If there's a single question raised by this recent Public Agenda study, it is, "What price perfection?" Or, to put it another way, has the professors' strategy for education become a riveting example of letting the perfect be the enemy of the good?

Education professors argue passionately for an approach to teaching that will nurture inquiring, curious minds that are open to new information, capable of solving problems, and respectful of different points of view and alternative paths for getting from here to there. Surely no one could fault this premise, and virtually every group (however much they may argue about other matters) agrees that love of learning is a worthy goal. But while others acknowledge the professors' vision, most of the professors themselves seem remarkably dismissive of the educational concerns of nearly everybody else.

> **Is there a point when a visionary agenda is so detached from daily concerns that it becomes counterproductive?**

OUTMODED BELIEFS

Most typical Americans – along with most employers – are alarmed by the number of youngsters they see who lack even basic skills, particularly such fundamentals as spelling and grammar. But for education professors, training teachers who stress correct English usage is a distinctly low priority. Typical Americans – given the dismal skills they see among many of today's students – wonder whether new teaching techniques really produce reliable educational results. But most professors discount such concerns, characterizing the public's views on teaching as "outmoded and mistaken." We want more parent involvement, the professors seem to be saying, as long as parents and taxpayers are brought up to speed.

FEW TANGIBLE STAKES

The public has voiced repeated concerns about discipline in the schools, and teachers often talk painfully about their struggles to maintain orderly classrooms and cope with rowdy, disruptive students. But once again, most professors of education consider this a low-level problem. Teacher education programs, by their report, give scant attention to the challenges of managing an unruly classroom. Teachers, the professors seem to say, could resolve their problems if they would just create more engaging lesson plans based upon more active learning.

Reformers, elected officials, and concerned business leaders have called for more rigorous academic standards and more accountability, and the professors say they too support higher standards and expectations. But they seem reluctant to attach any tangible stakes to student achievement or to consent to any viable means of measuring it. They distrust most forms of testing and quickly back away from any action that smacks of a negative sanction.

ADULTS DON'T CARE

As we analyzed the results of this study, I frequently recalled how poignantly the teenagers we interviewed for our earlier *Getting By* report yearned for order, structure, accountability, and moral authority in their lives. I remember their evocation of a rough and coarse environment in which no one seems to notice how flagrant cheating is or whether homework is turned in on time. Seeing some classmates consistently violate the rules and get away with it or repeatedly disrupt their classes and go right on doing it, sent a shockingly clear signal to many teens: Adults don't really care what we do. But professors of education have little to say about all this, with most acknowledging that they have not been in a classroom for more than 15 years.

Yet even as they tenaciously hold onto their own view of the practice of education, the professors voice doubts about whether their programs, their teachers-in-training, or they themselves are up to the task. Roughly 3 in 4 professors say they sometimes or often come across students whom they seriously doubt have what it takes to be good teachers.

UNQUESTIONABLY RIGHT?

My point here is not to play the all-too-frequent game of blame-shifting, nor to suggest that the professors' idealism about learning does not have an important message within it. But the disconnect between what the professors want and what most parents, teachers, and students say they need is often staggering. It seems ironic that so many of those who profess to believe that "the real endeavor" is about questioning and learning how to learn are seemingly entrapped in a mind-set that is unquestioning in its conviction of its own rightness.

To hold onto a goal that one believes is worthwhile is an important mission. But isn't it also fair to ask teachers of teachers to listen more empathetically to both the public's and the teachers' concerns? Isn't it time education professors began a dialogue which acknowledges that the testimony of parents and teachers and employers and students may have something of value in it?

But the disconnect between what the professors want and what most parents, teachers, and students say they need is often staggering.

As with other Public Agenda studies, I believe that *Different Drummers* poses a challenging question for those who want to improve the schools – one we cannot afford to ignore any longer. How can we possibly serve the nation's children well if more than 100,000 graduates of education programs – nursed by their professors' vision – enter the nation's classrooms each year prepared for an ideal, but unarmed for the reality?

Deborah Wadsworth

TABLE 1

Question: Teacher education programs can impart different qualities to their students and I want to ask which qualities you think are most essential and which are least essential. Please use a 1 to 5 scale, where 1 means it is least essential and 5 means it is absolutely essential to impart.

% responding item is "absolutely essential"	
Teachers who are themselves life-long learners and constantly updating their skills	84%
Teachers committed to teaching kids to be active learners who know how to learn	82
Teachers who will have high expectations of all their students	72
Teachers who are deeply knowledgeable about the content of the specific subjects they will be teaching	57
Teachers who are well-versed in theories of child development and learning	46
Teachers prepared to teach in schools with limited resources and where many kids come to class not ready to learn	45
Teachers trained in pragmatic issues of running a classroom such as managing time and preparing lesson plans	41
Teachers who maintain discipline and order in the classroom	37
Teachers who stress correct spelling, grammar, and punctuation	19
Teachers who expect students to be neat, on time, and polite	12

Note: Rounding may cause slight discrepancies between numbers in tables and numbers in the text.

TABLE 2

Question: We know that these are complicated issues and that many of the following views on teacher education will vary from school to school. When responding, please think in general terms and tell me how close each comes to your own view. [Insert item] Is that very close, somewhat close, not too close, or not close at all to your view?

% responding item is "very close" or "somewhat close"	
Teacher education programs need to do a better job weeding out students who are unsuitable for the profession	86%
Most professors of education need to spend more time in K-12 classrooms	84
Teacher education programs are often unfairly blamed for the problems facing public education	82
Teaching programs and professors of education are often treated as second-class citizens within the higher education system	79
Teacher education programs produce good teachers, but pressure and lack of support in many schools make it difficult for classroom teachers to succeed	79
Too many education students have trouble writing essays free of mistakes in grammar and spelling	75
Teacher education programs are loaded down with outdated requirements and state mandates that stand in the way of good teaching	63
Teacher education programs often fail to prepare teachers for the challenges of teaching in the real world	63
When a public school teacher faces a disruptive class, it probably means he or she has failed to make lessons engaging enough to the students	61
Teacher education programs are too often seen as cash cows by university administrators	54
Great teachers are born, not made	33

TABLE 3

Question: Thinking about the typical K – 12 classroom, would you like to see more, less or about the same use of the following learning tools?

% responding:	more	less
Portfolios and other authentic assessments	78%	5%
Computer programs that enable kids to practice skills on their own	69	7
Mixed ability grouping	50	15
Homework assignments	41	13
Penalties for students who break the rules	37	15
Homogenous grouping	15	54
Memorization	14	60
Prizes to reward good behavior in the classroom	13	52
Multiple-choice exams	2	78

TABLE 4

Question: How much emphasis do you or does your teacher education program place on teaching prospective teachers how to do the following, a lot, some, a little, or none at all?

% responding "a lot" of emphasis	
Teaching kids from diverse ethnic and cultural backgrounds	54%
Identifying students with learning disabilities	43
Teaching prospective teachers to manage a rowdy classroom	30
Communicating with parents	27
Identifying gifted students	15
Handling cheating or lying by students	8

TABLE 5

Question: Some people say there is a core body of knowledge that includes great literature, such as Shakespeare, and important historical documents, such as the Constitution, that the public schools and teachers must teach. Here are different views on this issue, please tell us how closely each comes to your own view. [Insert item] Is that very close, somewhat close, not too close, or not close at all to your view?

% responding item is "very close" or "somewhat close"	
It is critical for kids to gain a common, shared understanding of this core body of knowledge because it has defined our culture	77%
Any student who receives a high school diploma without being exposed to this core body of knowledge has been cheated in a fundamental way	76
Designating a core body of knowledge amounts to unfairly imposing one group's cultural values on others	37
Emphasizing a core body of knowledge would needlessly distract teachers from their most important goal, teaching kids how to learn	34
Since there is no consensus on what constitutes this core body of knowledge, teachers cannot be expected to teach it	30

TABLE 6

Question: Here are some perceptions about the nation's public schools. How close does each come to your own view? [Insert item] Is that very close, somewhat close, not too close, or not at all close to your own view?

% responding item is "very close" or "somewhat close"	
Public education is the nation's most critical democratic institution and should be protected at all costs	95%
The schools are expected to deal with too many social problems	85
The general public has outmoded and mistaken beliefs about what good teaching means	79
Even when the schools get more money, it often does not get to the classrooms	78
Academic standards in today's schools are too low and kids are not expected to learn enough	78
Too many school systems are top heavy with bureaucracy and administration	77
The schools should pay very careful attention to what business wants from high school graduates	75
Considering the differences in the children they teach, private schools don't do a better job than the public ones	67
Much of the decline in public confidence in public schools is a result of negative press coverage	65
Too many kids get passed on to the next grade when they should be held back	61
One of the most effective ways to improve the schools is to give them a lot more money	54
Many of the criticisms of the public schools come from right-wing groups who want to undermine public education	54
More often than not, teacher tenure is an obstacle to improving the schools	52
Most of the problems facing schools today are confined to urban school systems	22

TABLE 7

Question: I am going to read you some ideas for changing the way public schools teach. For each, I'd like you to tell me if you think it would improve kids' academic achievement. Please use a 1 to 5 scale, where 1 means it would not improve academic achievement at all and 5 means it would improve academic achievement a great deal.

% giving item a "4" or "5" rating	EDUCATION PROFESSORS	K – 12 TEACHERS	GENERAL PUBLIC
Emphasizing such work habits as being on time, dependable, and disciplined	78%	93%	88%
Not allowing kids to graduate from high school unless they clearly demonstrate they can write and speak English well	76	83	88
Setting up very clear guidelines on what kids should learn and the teachers should teach in every major subject, so the kids and the teachers will know what to aim for	71	80	82
Taking persistent troublemakers out of class so that teachers can concentrate on the kids who want to learn	66	88	73
Permanently removing from school grounds kids who are caught with drugs or with weapons	66	84	76
Replacing multiple-choice tests with essays to measure what kids learn	60	47	54
Mixing fast learners and slow learners in the same class so that slower kids learn from faster kids	54	40	34
Raising the standards of promotion from grade school to junior high and only letting kids move ahead when they pass a test showing they have reached those standards	49	62	70
Adapting how schools teach to the background of students, such as using street language to teach inner-city kids	18	15	20

Different Drummers is based on a telephone survey of 900 randomly selected professors of education who work in colleges and universities throughout the continental United States. Prior to the survey, Public Agenda senior staff interviewed ten experts in the field of teacher education and conducted four focus groups with professors of education across the country.

THE TELEPHONE SURVEY

Interviews with 900 professors of education were conducted by phone between July 9 and September 5, 1997. The margin of error for the sample is plus or minus 3%. Interviews averaged 47 minutes in length. The survey instrument (questionnaire) was designed by Public Agenda.

The final sample was derived in the following way. A proportionate random sample of 5,324 teacher educators was drawn from a universe of approximately 34,000 teacher educators including deans, chairpersons, and faculty members from colleges and universities with departments of education that offer a bachelor's degree or higher. Each of the teacher educators was contacted at his or her school by mail in May 1997 and invited to participate in the survey. The invitation letter requested information such as the telephone number where respondents could best be reached and their availability for a telephone interview during the summer; a business reply envelope was provided to facilitate responses. Telephone interviews were conducted at times designated as most convenient for respondents. In addition, respondents were given a toll-free number they could call at any time – including evenings and weekends – to conduct the interview. The number of interviews executed through this process was 778. These were supplemented with an additional 122 interviews completed by calling teacher educators directly at their places of work at the end of August and during the first week of September.

As in all surveys, question order effects and other non-sampling sources of error can sometimes affect results. Steps were taken to minimize these, including pre-testing the survey instrument and randomizing the order in which some questions were asked.

Sample was supplied by Market Data Retrieval (MDR) of Shelton, Connecticut. Robinson and Muenster Associates, Inc., of Sioux Falls, South Dakota conducted the interviews.

THE FOCUS GROUPS

Focus groups allow for an in-depth, qualitative exploration of the dynamics underlying attitudes toward complex issues. Insights from these groups were important to the survey design, and quotes were drawn from them to give voice to attitudes captured statistically through the survey interviews.

The focus groups were conducted in New York, Chicago, Boston, and Los Angeles. The participants were teacher educators – both professors and administrators – working in teacher education programs in four-year colleges and universities in each of the cities. In all cases, local professional market research organizations recruited participants to Public Agenda's specifications. All focus groups were moderated by Public Agenda senior staff.

THE EXPERT INTERVIEWS

Public Agenda interviewed ten experts in the field to obtain a grounding in the current substantive issues concerning teacher education. These interviews, conducted via telephone in May 1997, included deans and professors in departments of education in schools across the country, as well as several leaders of associations and organizations involved with higher education and teacher preparation.

ENDNOTES

1. *Getting By: What American Teenagers Really Think About Their Schools* (Public Agenda, 1997), p. 42, p. 44.

2. Eighty-six percent of the public, and 73% of teachers, want students to memorize the multiplication tables and do math by hand before using calculators. Source: *Given the Circumstances: Teachers Talk About Public Education Today* (Public Agenda, 1996), p. 19.

3. *Divided Within, Besieged Without: The Politics of Education in Four American School Districts* (Public Agenda, 1993), ps. 8-9.

4. *Given the Circumstances,* p. 16, p. 41.

5. Seventy-one percent of high school students state "too many disruptive students" is a serious problem in their schools, and 68% identify cheating on tests and assignments as a serious problem. Source: *Getting By,* p. 15, p. 34, p. 42.

6. *First Things First: What Americans Expect from the Public Schools* (Public Agenda, 1994), p. 11, p. 13, p. 41.

7. Forty-seven percent of the public surveyed responded that they do not believe a high school degree is a guarantee that a student has learned the basics. Source: *Assignment Incomplete, The Unfinished Business of Education Reform* (Public Agenda, 1995), p. 19.

8. When high school students were asked to talk about different kinds of teachers, 71% responded they would learn a lot more from "a teacher who is enthusiastic and excited about the subject they teach" with only 29% responding that most of their teachers are like that now. Sixty-seven percent responded that they would learn a lot more from "a teacher who uses hands-on projects and class discussion" and only 22% responded that most of their teachers are like that now. Source: *Getting By,* p. 49.

9. *Getting By,* p. 45.

10. *Getting By,* p. 43.

11. Ninety-two percent of the public thinks it is either an "excellent" or "good" idea that schools should place much greater emphasis on making learning enjoyable and interesting to elementary school students, and 86% think it is either an "excellent" or "good" idea for high school students. Source: *First Things First,* p. 21, p. 43.

12. *Given the Circumstances,* p. 20.

13. Ethan Bronner, "End of Chicago's Education School Stirs Debate," *New York Times,* 9/17/97, A27.

14. Ninety-two percent of the public think basic reading, writing, and math skills are "absolutely essential" for local schools to be teaching. Forty-seven percent say they do not believe a high school degree is a guarantee that a student has learned the basics. Source: *Assignment Incomplete,* p. 19.

15. *First Things First,* p. 15, p. 42.

Kids These Days: What Americans Really Think About The Next Generation. 1997. A comprehensive study of Americans' attitudes toward our nation's youth, including a special focus on the views of black, Hispanic and white parents. Will today's children, once grown, make this country a better place? Are parents teaching their kids right from wrong? What solutions do Americans propose to the problems children face? These questions, and what kids have to say, are addressed in this study. Copies available from Public Agenda for $10.00.

Getting By: What American Teenagers Really Think About Their Schools. 1997. Public high school students are the focus of this national telephone survey, which looks at how teens view their schools, teachers, and the learning process. Includes insights into what students say would motivate them to work harder in school and how they define "good" and "bad" teaching. Special sections on black and Hispanic students, private high school students, and students from Jefferson County (KY) and the San Francisco Bay Area are included. Copies are available from Public Agenda for $10.00.

Our Nation's Kids: Is Something Wrong? 1997. A new National Issues Forums book that focuses on the problems today's young people are facing. Three approaches that have wide public support are explored. Copies are available from Kendall/Hunt, (800) 228-0810.

Given the Circumstances: Teachers Talk About Public Education Today. 1996. Focuses on how public school teachers view the performance of the public schools; what children need to learn; and what schools need to be effective. A special focus on black and Hispanic teachers is included, along with a comparison of the views of teachers, the public, parents, and community leaders. Copies are available from Public Agenda for $10.00.

Assignment Incomplete: The Unfinished Business of Education Reform. 1995. A follow-up study to *First Things First* (1994), this report examines why public support for public schools is in jeopardy; why **Americans** are so focused on the basics; whether people are really committed to higher standards; and whether **they** value education in and of itself. Copies are available from Public Agenda for $10.00.

First Things First: What Americans Expect from the Public Schools. 1994. Looks at how the general public, including parents of children currently in public schools, views education reform efforts as well as values issues in the schools. Included are detailed analyses of the perspectives of white and black public school parents, as well as parents identified as traditional Christians. Copies are available from Public Agenda for $10.00.

Professional Development for Teachers: The Public's View. 1995. Examines the potential for both public support and disappointment with professional development for teachers. Copies are available from Public Agenda for $7.50.

Good News, Bad News: What People Really Think About The Education Press. 1997. Prepared for the Education Writers Association, this study explores the attitudes of the general public, parents with children in public schools, educators, and education reporters and editors, toward media coverage of education. Copies are available from Public Agenda for $7.00.

Americans' Views on Standards: An Assessment by Public Agenda. 1996. Prepared for the 1996 Education Summit, this assessment draws from Public Agenda's extensive archive of public opinion research on education – including surveys and focus group reports – and from studies by other prominent opinion analysts. Copies are available from Public Agenda for $7.50.

What Our Children Need: South Carolinians Look at Public Education. 1997. Prepared for the South Carolina Department of Education, this comprehensive study examines how South Carolinians view their public schools. The differences among the public, educators and community leaders in how they look at their schools and what solutions they feel are most promising are identified. Copies are available from the South Carolina Department of Education, (800) 765-KIDS (in state) or (803) 734-5742.

Committed to Change: Missouri Citizens and Public Education. 1996. Prepared by Public Agenda for The Missouri Partnership for Outstanding Schools, this report describes how Missouri citizens feel about public education. Gaps in perspectives among educators, community leaders, and the public, including a special focus on blacks, are outlined. Copies of the report are available from The Missouri Partnership for Outstanding Schools, 920A E. Broadway, Suite #203, Columbia, MO 65201-4858, (800) 659-4044.

The Broken Contract: Connecticut Citizens Look at Public Education. 1994. Prepared by Public Agenda for the William Caspar Graustein Memorial Fund, this study describes how the citizens of Connecticut feel about public education and integration in their state and why they hold these attitudes. The gaps among educators, business leaders, and the public, including a special focus on blacks and Hispanics, are outlined. Copies are available from Public Agenda for $5.50.

Divided Within, Besieged Without: The Politics of Education in Four American School Districts. 1993. Prepared by Public Agenda for the Kettering Foundation, this study of educators, education administrators, parents, and business executives looks at the substantial in-fighting and communication gaps among these groups of education stakeholders. Copies are available from Public Agenda for $10.00.

Unless otherwise indicated reports can be ordered by calling or writing Public Agenda at 6 East 39th Street, New York, NY 10016; tel: (212) 686-6610; fax: (212) 889-3461; online: http://www.publicagenda.org. Shipping and handling costs will be applied.

PUBLIC AGENDA
6 EAST 39TH STREET
NEW YORK, NY 10016

TEL 212.686.6610
FAX 212.889.3461
www.publicagenda.org

Price: $10.00
ISBN 1-889483-47-8